My Yum

by Wiley Blevins

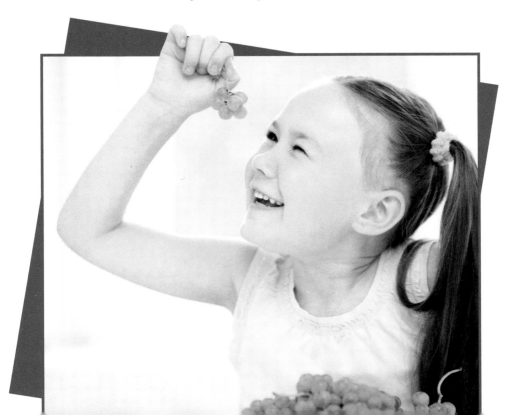

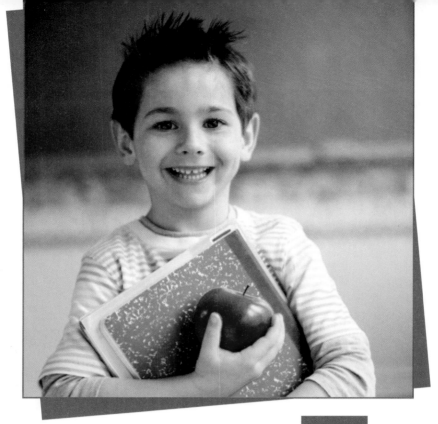

My apple is red .

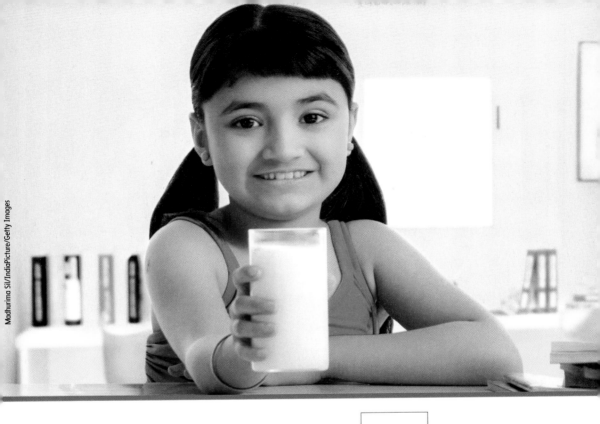

My milk is ⬜ .
white

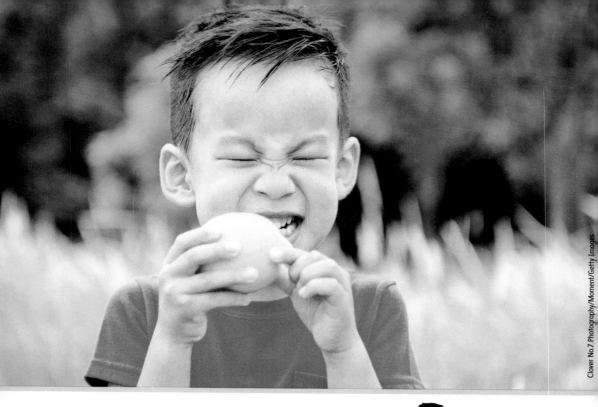

My lemon is sour .

Clover No.7 Photography/Moment/Getty Images

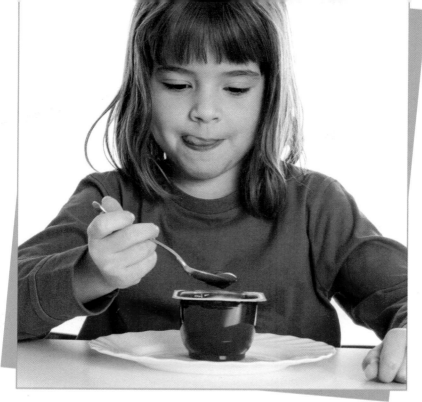

My pudding is sweet .

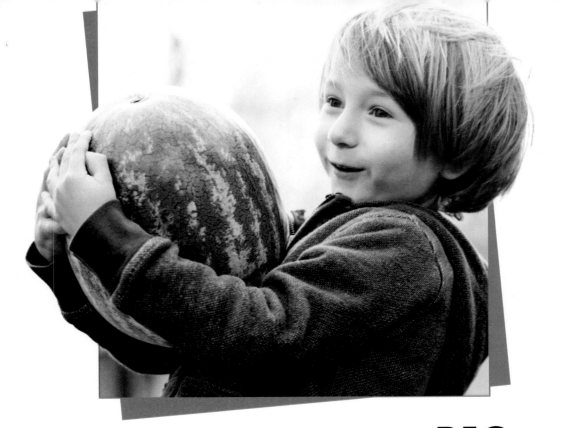

My watermelon is BIG.

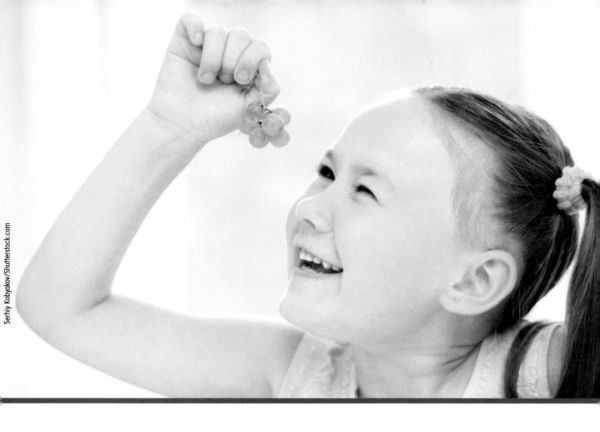

My grape is little.

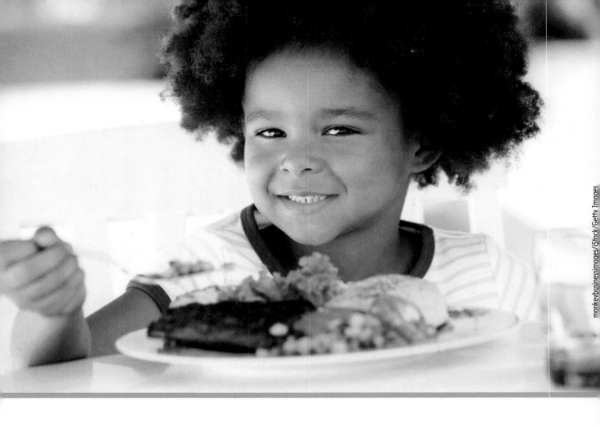

My food is yummy!